Deanis V Rita

Happy Christmas
2001

With much love
from us all

A, G, I, O, A

X

It can only happen to a golfer

Chris Plumridge

Illustrations by
John Ireland

Queen Anne Press

A Queen Anne Press Book

First published in Great Britain in 1999 by
Queen Anne Press, a division of
Lennard Associates Limited
Mackerye End, Harpenden
Herts AL5 5DR

A CIP catalogue record for this book
is available from the British Library

ISBN 1 85291 615 X

Cover design: Paul Cooper

Printed and bound in Slovenia

introduction

Most golfers will tell you that they play the game for the challenge it presents, the company it provides and the fresh air and exercise that is always available.

While these are valid points, the truth is that golfers are among the most deluded of sportsmen and women, clinging to the belief that no matter how badly they perform, tomorrow it will be better. Invariably, it isn't and accepting this fact is part and parcel of finding peace and eternal happiness on the golf course.

If there is a game where Sod's Law plays a bigger role, I have yet to discover it. The propensity for golf balls to find the

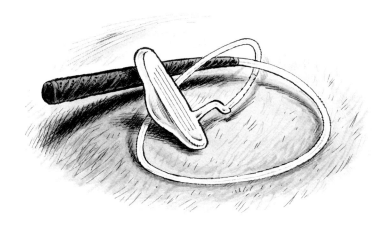

most outlandish places, the myriad of rules and definitions, the technical jargon and the clashing of cultures mean that things are always going to go wrong, and even if they can't, they might.

This book has been created to highlight those areas where fate is ready to deliver the sand-filled sock to the base of the skull and point out, in a series of pithy maxims and truisms, the things that can only happen to a golfer.

Chris Plumridge

the only simple thing
about golf is that it is
relatively easy to spell.

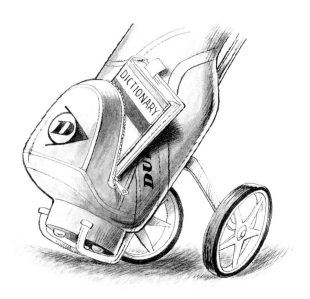

people who say it's the one good shot in a round that will bring you back for the next time haven't had to put up with the other 98 bad shots.

in golf, you're always learning something new, even if it's that you'll never be any good at it.

most golfers have delusions of adequacy.

another name

for golf is

'disappointment'.

the pencil needed to mark a card is always at the bottom of the bag. And when it is found, it is broken.

golfers who know the rules backwards are to be avoided.

par figures that appear printed on the card are rarely copied by hand.

---

someone always says 'One'
when your ball falls off the tee peg.
The same person always says 'never up,
never in' when you leave a putt of three
feet short. The same person always
says 'Why didn't you do that the first
time' when you hit a rasping stroke with
a provisional ball. The same person has
to be led away before you fell him with
your sand-wedge.

passing lorry-drivers always shout 'Fore' at the top of your backswing.

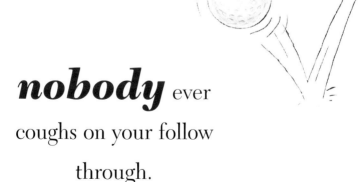

nobody ever coughs on your follow through.

---

the first tee
shot following a lesson
travels 20 yards along the
ground.

in a pro-am, you are the
last to drive off after your professional
and partners have all hit screamers.

using an old ball for a shot over water does not mean you will avoid the splash.

the more you play a course the more obsessed you become with its dangers.

when there is one minute left to get to the first tee, a shoelace breaks.

the only available space in the car park is always furthest from the locker-room.

when you drive your car to a pro-am, you are caught in an impenetrable traffic jam.

while unloading your golf bag from the car, the golf balls fall out all over the tarmac car park and roll under the other cars.

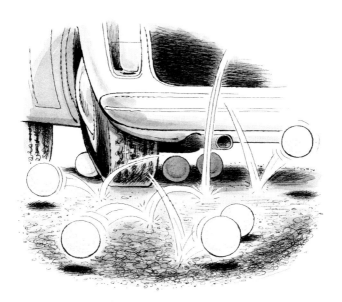

the most important inches in golf are not those between the ears: they are the ones between your ball and the hole on the fourth putt.

---

greens are hollow-tined and dressed the day before a competition.

the 'yips' is something that afflicts other people. Until now.

the shorter the putt, the smaller the hole becomes.

---

the newer the golf ball the more likely you are to lose it.

if a good course is one where you play to your handicap or better and a bad course is one where you struggle to break 100, why are there so many bad courses?

all forms of wildlife on a golf

course are there for the express

purpose of putting

you off.

electric

trolleys always break down at the

furthest point from the clubhouse.

the waiting-list at

the Club you wish to join has just

closed.

the captain

of the Club you wish to join turns out to

be someone you were at school with:

and you never got on.

the club

secretary is always on the
course when you want
him, but is in the bar
when your sub is overdue.

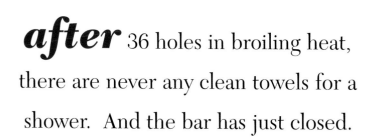

after 36 holes in broiling heat,
there are never any clean towels for a
shower. And the bar has just closed.

the sand in the bunkers is
never the right texture for your
particular technique.

---

bunkers have the unnerving habit of rushing out to meet your ball.

when you play a shot from a bunker and the ball hits the bank, there is a split second when you have no idea as to the ball's whereabouts before it plummets down on your foot.

---

when you can tear yourself away from the office for a rare mid-week round you find yourself in the midst of a visiting society.

it's always the next round that will find you playing your normal game.

*if **you*** have a hole-in-one in a competition you are in the last group and the bar is packed when you come in.

short holes are never as short as you think.

if you find your ball in the woods, it is unplayable. If a professional finds his ball in woods, not only is it playable but he can hit it onto the green.

your best drive of the day finishes in a divot hole.

the people in front of you are playing too slowly, the people behind you are playing too quickly.

your greatest round takes place against an important business contact whom you can't afford to humiliate.

---

the number of practice balls recovered is always less than the number hit.

if you have difficulty meeting new people, try picking up someone else's golf ball.

whenever you take your clubs on holiday, you leave your game behind.

if you're out in 39 and home in 45 you're playing war-time golf.

---

the shortest

distance between the ball

and the target is never a

straight line.

when playing to a

temporary green, your ball finishes

stone dead to the hole cut in the proper

green.

if there is one solitary tree
located on a hole, your ball will find it
with unerring accuracy.

shots that finish close to the pin
are never as close when you get there.

---

immediately

you put on your

waterproofs it stops

raining.

waterproof trousers

cannot be removed without falling over.

the reserve

glove you have kept for

wet weather has

shrunk.

---

in a match,

younger golfers always

have your measure … so

do older golfers for that

matter.

in most medal rounds, you

start badly then fade away.

if you are playing well in a competition, your partner will tell you that if you keep it up you must win. This remark ensures that you finish with a string of double-bogeys.

your best medal round of the year is one shot too many to win the competition.

---

the fact

that trees are ninety per cent air does

not mean your ball will avoid the

remaining ten

per cent of

timber.

people who say a shank is

close to a perfect shot have never had

four in a row.

your controlled draw rapidly develops into a chronic hook: similarly, your controlled fade is, in reality, a vicious slice.

hitting an iron off the tee for safety means same direction, less distance.

golf is like sex: afterwards you feel you should have scored a little better.

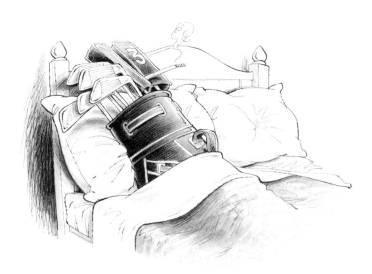

foursomes golf means

always having to say you're sorry.

the love of your life either

hates golf or is a better player than you.

handicaps

are designed to keep you

in your place.

teeing up on the side nearest the out-of-bounds means your ball will finish in the cabbage on the other side.

---

no successive

swings are ever the same except when you hit consecutive shots out of bounds.

there is no truth in the theory

that if you know how to shank you will never do so.

out-of-bounds fences

are located a foot the wrong side of your ball.

if the club is burgled, your clubs are never stolen. And if they are, you are under-insured.

coincidentally the only remaining set of clubs in the professional's shop was made especially for you.

your natural ability as a golfer is in inverse proportion to the amount of money you spend on new equipment.

the hickory-shafted driver that you found in your grandmother's attic turns out to be worth only £10.

the ball

nestling in a footprint in a

bunker is

invariably

yours.

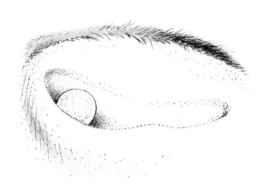

whatever the rule for a

particular situation, you've probably

broken it.

---

the distant puff of sand
you see means that your ball has not
carried the bunker and what's more, it
is plugged under the lip.

delicate chip
shots over bunkers always
catch the top of the bank
and fall back.

---

the first time
you enter the club's
knockout competition you
are drawn against the
club champion in the first
round.

in a four-ball game, your partner is
right on his game while you aren't, or
vice versa.

golf is the only game in which you fail to win 99 per cent of the time.

if you are giving strokes in a match it's always too many: if you are receiving them it's never enough.

spike marks always
deflect your ball away from the hole.

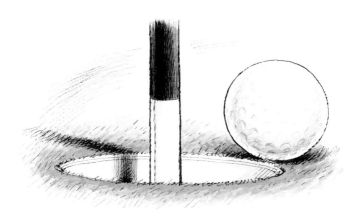

curly, downhill, left-to-right putts are usually followed by curly, uphill, right-to-left putts.

lagging a putt from three feet means you've got the yips.

always concede the fourth putt.

---

your first

hole-in-one is always

achieved when playing

alone.

during the first

round with a brand new

set of clubs, the ball has

to be played from a road.

finding the key
to a better game means
opening a lot of
doors.

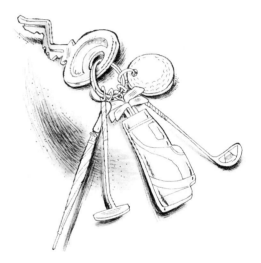

the only downwind holes are
par threes.

when you are looking for your ball, it is found (a) when you have trudged back and put another ball in play, (b) when the five minutes search time has elapsed, (c) when you tread on it and incur a penalty.

---

keeping your head down means you'll be looking at a very large divot.

if a golfer wishes to give you a blow-by-blow account of his round, ask him to start with his final putt on the 18th green.

a vacuum is the space between your ears that becomes entirely void of matter once you set foot on the course.

curing the faults in your swing
can never be affected in just one lesson
from a professional.

your favourite
golf sweater is the one that gets
shrunk in the
wash.

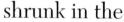

a golf gift given to you at Christmas by a non-golfer is always unsuitable.

the latest piece of written instruction never works on the course.

Quote from Christy O'Connor:

'If it wasn't my living, I wouldn't play golf if you paid me.'

In practice ⟫ 57 – 102

Find out ⟫ 103 – 125

Credits

P.12-13 The flight of Orville Wright (c) Roger Viollet collection - **P. 14,** Advertisement for the Zeppelin (c) G. Namur/Explorer - **P. 17,** Poster for the Farman by Albert Solon, 1926, Arts Déco Library (c) J.-L. Charmet/Explorer - **P. 18,** Ellen Church (c) Roger Viollet collection - **P. 20,** In a plane, 1936 (c) Mary Evans/Explorer - **P. 23,** A plan for an airport (c) J.-L. Charmet/Explorer - **P. 25,** DC-6 (c) Superstock - **P. 26,** Engines of a Boeing 747 (c) Paul Chesley/Fotogram-Stone Images -

P. 29, Passengers on board the Comet (c) Tonystone - **P. 30,** Comet (c) Tonystone - **P. 32-33,** Caravelle landing (c) Bauer collection/Explorer - **P. 34,** Concorde (c) Radenne/Explorer **P. 36,** Nose of a Boeing 747 - (c) Mark R. Wagner/Fotogram-Stone Images - **P. 38,** A3XX (c) Airbus Industrie - **P. 40-41,** Roissy airport (c) Henry Raguet/IDPress.net - **P. 42-3,** Control tower (c) Henry Raguet/IDPress.net - **P. 44,** Loading freight (c) Henry Raguet/IDPress.net - **P.45** Loading a cargo plane (c) Henry Raguet/IDPress.net **P. 46-7,** On the runways (c) Henry Raguet/IDPress.net **P. 48,** Loading baggage (c) Henry Raguet/IDPress.net **P. 49,** Sorting packages (c) Henry Raguet/IDPress.net **P. 50-51,** The peninsula at Roissy (c) Henry Raguet/IDPress.net **P. 52-3** Terminal 2F (c) Henry Raguet/IDPress.net **P. 54,** Pilots preparing for their flight (c) Henry Raguet/IDPress.net **P. 55,** Maintenance of the lights (c) Henry Raguet/IDPress.net **P. 56,** (c) Henry Raguet/IDPress.net **P. 58-59,** computer graphics: Jacques Partouche **P. 60-61,** computer graphics: /Fabrice Mathé/Altedia Press **P.62-3,** computer graphics: Roger Rivet **P. 64-6** by kind permission of Air France magazine, the in-flight magazine of Air France and (c) Iberia, Alitalia, British Airways, Lufthansa, Swissair, Air Littoral - **P.68-9** (c) Air France, Communications department **P. 70-71,** computer graphics: Jacques Partouche - **P. 71-3,** KLM and by kind permission of Air France Magazine **P. 74-75,** computer graphics: Fabrice Mathé/Altedia **P. 76-91,** computer graphics: Jacques Partouche **P. 91,** computer graphics: Fabrice Mathé/Altedia **P. 96-7,** computer graphics: Jacques Partouche **P. 98-99,** model : Christelle Mekdjian/Altedia - **P. 100-102,** computer graphics: Jacques Partouche **P. 104-5,** Illustrations : Phong Luong Dien - **P. 106-107,** Planescape by Erro', 1970 (c) André Morain/Erro' - **P. 108-109,** (c) British Airways and (c) ANA **P. 110-11,** A3XX (c) Airbus Industrie - **P.114-21,** illustrations: Phong Luong Dien.

Acknowledgements

We are grateful to the following for their kind assistance: Corinne Bélière, Laurence Benette, Jean-Marie Dano/Altedia, Michel Devos, Violaine Gérard, Jacques Girerd, Martine Marillier, Air France and COMUTA.